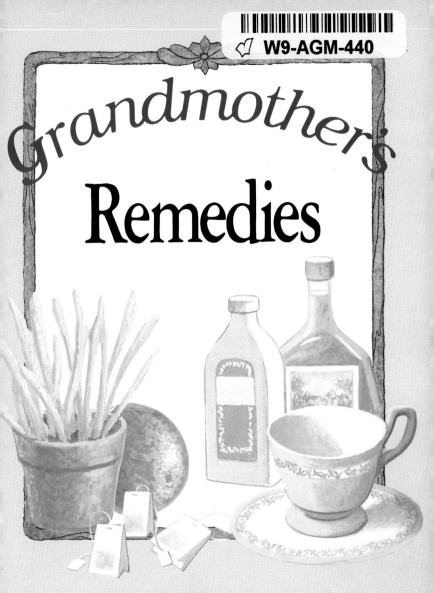

Grandmother's

Remedies

Written by Marian Hoffman

AVENEL
New York

Created and manufactured for Avenel
by Ottenheimer Publishers, Inc.
Copyright © 1991 Ottenheimer Publishers, Inc.
All rights reserved
This 1991 edition published by Avenel, distributed by
Outlet Book Company, Inc., a Random House Company,
225 Park Avenue South, New York, New York 10003

Printed and bound in Italy

ISBN 0-517-03741-6

8 7 6 5 4 3 2 1

Contents

Natural Refreshers

I do a great deal of sewing and suffer from tired, strained eyes at the end of the day. I use a number of tricks to refresh my eyes, but my favorite cure for tired eyes is a rosemary tea soak.

1 teaspoon dried rosemary or 1
    rosemary tea bag
1 cup boiling water

Place the rosemary in the water and steep for 10 minutes. Dip a cotton pad in the tea and place over the eyes for 15 minutes.

A compress made from damp camomile tea bags helps eliminate puffy eyes. Wet the tea bags with lukewarm or cool water and place them on the puffy area for 15 minutes.

Cucumbers and potatoes are helpful in treating strained and inflamed eyes. You'll be surprised at how cooling and soothing a cucumber slice resting on your closed eyelids for 15 minutes can be. Keeping a thin slice of a raw red potato on your closed eyelids for at least 20 minutes will also banish that tired, achy feeling.

Herbal Baths

Nothing is as relaxing and refreshing as an herbal bath. You can easily prepare an herbal bath by placing a handful of fresh or dried herbs in the center of a cloth handkerchief. Pull the handkerchief up around the herbs to form a small bag and fasten tightly. Place the bag in the tub and fill the tub with water. After the bath, spread the herbs out to dry—they can be reused 2 or 3 times.

Camomile, alfalfa, and rose are particularly helpful for dry skin. Catnip, sage, and camomile are good herbs to use for relaxation. Herbal baths also help relieve the pain of aching muscles and increase circulation. One of the best herbs for this purpose is ginger. Drop a few granules of grated ginger into a tub of warm water and relax in the tub.

Try adding a pint of corn, safflower, olive, or peanut oil to 1/2 ounce of herbs to make a pleasant, therapeutic bath oil.

Another way to pamper your skin is to pour a pint of milk, lemon slices, or the juice of a large grapefruit into a tub of warm water.

Essential oils can be used to make a delightful cleansing bath oil. Sage oil works wonders for aching muscles. Jasmine, sandalwood, and rose oils are relaxing, while mint oils are stimulating.

Poultices

Herb poultices can sooth the discomfort of burns, bites, and skin inflammations. Wrap fresh or dried herbs that are powdered or have been softened in hot water in a clean cloth handkerchief. Moisten the poultice and place on the affected area. Cover with a warm cloth or hold in place with an elastic bandage. When the poultice dries out, make a new poultice using a clean handkerchief.

Different herbs are helpful for different conditions. A comfrey poultice helps heal fractures, insect bites, and burns. A camomile poultice relieves the pain of an earache. If I have no loose camomile available, I make the poultice with damp camomile tea bags. Black mustard poultices help relieve chest congestion or painful rheumatism.

A word of caution: This black mustard poultice, as with all herb poultices, can be irritating to sensitive skin. Try rubbing delicate skin with olive oil before applying the poultices.

Natural Dentrifices

I use a variety of home remedies to clean and freshen my teeth and mouth. My favorite is to squeeze the juice of fresh strawberries onto a cotton ball or a toothbrush and brush it over my teeth to make them shining white.

My neighbor shared this recipe for tooth powder with me:

1 ounce baking soda
1 ounce table salt
Powdered herbs of your choice, for
    flavor
1 drop essential oil, for scent

Combine the ingredients, stir well, and let sit for 2 or 3 hours. Add wintergreen if you want a minty taste; basil and rosemary can be added to improve circulation.

Press the mixture through a strainer. Store in a closed bottle.

Herbs are very useful for making your own mouthwash. If you drink sage, mint, or birch tea your breath will be fresher.

Mouthwash

$1/3$ teaspoon mint
$1/3$ teaspoon rosemary
$1/3$ teaspoon fennel seeds
1 cup boiling water

Combine the herbs and cover with the boiling water. Cover and steep for 10 minutes.

Strain the mixture and use to rinse your mouth.

Natural Pep

Some days it's hard to get going, and to keep going. Eating grapefruit in the morning is a good way to get your metabolism started. Squeeze out the juice of half a grapefruit, and add enough warm water to the juice to fill a 10-oz. glass. Slowly drink the liquid, then eat the fruit of the squeezed-out grapefruit half.

A glass of milk mixed with a tablespoon of blackstrap molasses also makes a good morning pick-me-up.

Some herbs are stimulants which, when used in moderation, can help combat fatigue. For more energy, drink a cup of ginseng tea. You can make your own ginseng tea by mixing ⅛ teaspoon of ginseng powder with a cup of hot water. This tea helps perk you up and overcomes feelings of mild depression.

Just cooling yourself off can be a great pick-me-up. Try placing cucumber peels over your face for a soothing, cooling feeling.

Refreshing Teas

Whenever I feel tense, upset, chilled, or generally run down, I make myself a comforting cup of tea. Herbal teas work wonders to relax and refresh you.

Packages of herb tea bags are available at grocery and natural food stores. Tea bags and loose tea should be stored in a container with a tightly fitting lid.

When using tea bags, keep the paper tags out of the water. This adds a paper taste to your delicious refresher.

Different herb teas help alleviate different problems. For example, mint tea freshens your breath, while camomile tea aids your digestion and helps induce sleep.

Sage, rosemary, basil, and alfalfa seed tea help reduce pain.

Sage tea also helps eliminate unpleasant body odors caused by nervous perspiration. Use 2 sage tea bags or 1½ teaspoons of dried sage for each cup of boiling water. Steep for 10 minutes and drink small amounts of the tea throughout the day.

Saffron tea and thyme tea, sweetened with honey, are reputed to chase away the blues. Save any leftover thyme tea to use as an insect repellant. Place the cold tea in a spray bottle and spritz it around your doors and windows to keep flies away. You can keep insects away from yourself by splashing camomile tea on your face and body.

Lotions & Moisturizers

In the winter particularly, I am always battling with dry, rough hands. An effective way to solve this problem is to soak your hands in warm water just before bedtime. Then rub pure glycerin into your hands and see how much softer they feel in the morning. Another treatment for dry, chapped hands is to place ½ teaspoon of sugar in the palm of your hand. Cover the sugar with baby oil and massage your hands together briskly for 3 or 4 minutes. Rinse your hands with warm, soapy water.

My mother always softened our skin with a lotion she made from rose water. She simmered rose petals in 3 cups of water for 10 minutes. Then she strained the liquid and added 1 cup of alcohol. Here is a variation of her rose water lotion:

1/4 cup rose water
1/4 cup rosemary tea
2 tablespoons egg white

Combine the ingredients in a blender or food processor. Store refrigerated, for up to 1 week.

Masks & Facials

There are a number of herb, vegetable, and fruit masks that help condition your skin.

Before applying a skin mask, make sure your skin is clean. A steam bath is the best way to deep-clean your face. Place 8 cups of water and 2 tablespoons of the herb of your choice in a pan and boil for 5 minutes. Pour the hot liquid into a large bowl. Make a tent over your head with a large towel and lean your face over the bowl for 5 to 10 minutes. Splash your face with cold water to close the pores. Now you are ready to apply a mask, making sure you avoid the delicate skin around the eyes.

For oily skin: Blend a quarter of a small, unpeeled eggplant and 1 cup of plain yogurt and process until well blended. Apply the mixture to your face and leave on for 20 minutes. Rinse off with warm water, then splash your face with cold water.

For dry skin: Blend 1 ripe avocado to a puree. Add an equal amount of sour cream. Apply the mixture to your face and leave it on for 15 minutes, then rinse off with warm water.

For combination skin: Peel a ripe papaya and blend to a puree. Pat the fruit puree on your face and neck. Leave on for 15 minutes, rinse with warm water, and splash your face and neck with cold water.

Cleansers & Skin Bracers

I find that store-bought soap is generally too drying to use on my face. Here is a way to make an ordinary bar of soap into a gentle, moisturizing cleanser.

1 bar store-bought soap
1/8 teaspoon honey
1/8 cup camomile or rose water

Chop up the bar of soap into a small pan. Add the honey and rose water and simmer until the soap melts. Cool and pour into a soap dispenser or plastic squeeze bottle.

Dry skin can also be cleaned gently with a mixture of 3 tablespoons of whole milk and 1/2 teaspoon of castor oil.

For oily skin, blend 1 teaspoon of powdered milk with ¼ cup of warm water. Apply to the skin with a cotton puff.

To tone skin, apply club soda or buttermilk to your face. Leave on for 10 minutes, then rinse with warm water.

Hair Conditioners & Rinses

One of the best conditioners I know for dry hair is mayonnaise. Massage 1/2 cup of mayonnaise into dry, unwashed hair. Cover the hair with a plastic bag and leave on for 15 minutes. Remove the bag, rinse several times, and shampoo well.

For oily hair, combine 4 cups of water with 4 teaspoons of spearmint leaves and bring to a boil. Cool and apply to your hair as an after-shampoo rinse.

Leftover tea makes a terrific after-shampoo rinse for brunettes, as does water containing several tablespoons of apple cider vinegar.

To get blonde hair shining, rinse with water containing 3 or 4 tablespoons of lemon juice.

To prevent split ends, try massaging a carton of plain yogurt into your hair. Comb the yogurt through, then rinse well.

Puree a cucumber adding little water if needed to make a smooth paste. Massage the cucumber into clean, towel-dried hair and leave for 10 minutes before rinsing well.

Do you have a problem with fly-away hair? Try mixing an egg with 6 tablespoons of plain yogurt. Shampoo, then briskly massage the mixture into your hair for 3 minutes. Cover with a towel for 10 minutes, then rinse with warm water.

Natural Shampoos

Clean, shining hair is an important part of a healthy appearance. My neighbor, who suffers from an allergy to regular shampoos, uses baking soda to wash her hair. She rubs a handful of dry baking soda into her wet hair, then rinses.

Washing with baking soda makes hair seem drier at first, but after a few weeks the hair becomes very soft.

It's also easy to make your own shampoo. Homemade shampoos won't be as sudsy as commercial ones, but they do a good job of cleaning.

Here is my shampoo recipe:

4 cups boiling water
1/2 cup castile soap flakes
4 to 8 drops essential oil
1 teaspoon isopropyl alcohol

Pour the boiling water over the
soap flakes, stirring until the soap
dissolves. To scent the shampoo,
dissolve the essential oil of any
herb you like in the alcohol. Add to
the soap mixture.

Natural Hair Coloring

Using herbs or vegetables, you can gradually lighten or darken your hair, or enrich your natural color.

Dried sage is the herb to darken brunette hair color and cover gray. Add 4 tablespoons of dried sage to 2 cups of just-boiled water. Steep for 2 to 3 hours, then strain. Pour the liquid over clean hair 15 times. After the last pour, let the hair dry naturally. Then rinse and dry the hair as usual. Apply this rinse weekly until the hair has reached the desired darkness, then use monthly to maintain the color.

To add golden highlights to blonde hair, combine 4 tablespoons of dried camomile with 2 cups of just-boiled water. Steep for 2 hours, then strain. Pour the liquid over clean hair 15 times. After the last pour, leave it in the hair for 15 minutes before rinsing with clear water. Try the same technique using a mixture of the juice of 2 lemons and a cup of warm water, being careful not to get the lemon juice on the skin. Sun dry hair after these rinses and the effects will be more apparent.

For redheads, combine 1 tablespoon each of henna, chamomile flowers, and vinegar with 3 cups of boiling water, and steep for 15 minutes. Strain and pour through the hair 15 times. After the last pour, leave in hair for 15 minutes, then rinse with clear water.

Personal Favorites

Dogs and cats have always been part of my family. I try hard to keep them brushed and washed, because I think cleanliness contributes to their general good health. To keep the animals well-groomed, I brush them daily to remove loose hair and dry skin. Once a month, I bathe them with my favorite soap formula, which makes their coats shining and helps deter fleas.

1 bar castile soap
1/3 cup strong rosemary tea

Grate the bar of soap, then melt it in a double boiler. Add the tea, stirring until well mixed. Pour the mixture into a container and cool until set.

If it is too difficult to give your pet a water bath, try rubbing baking soda into his coat and then brush it off. Baking soda is an effective deodorizer as well as cleanser.

If your dog sheds constantly, try lubricating his coat with a small amount of olive oil, coconut oil, or lanolin every 10 days.

Child Care Tips

There are innumerable crises that arise in the daily lives of small children. And, there are a number of little tricks that help minimize the trauma of these misadventures.

Band-aid removal: Children generally like having cuts covered with band-aids but can kick up a fuss when you must change it. Dip a piece of cotton in baby oil and rub it over the tape. The tape should pull up easily, without hurting the skin.

Medicines: Many liquid medicines taste so disagreeable that children dislike them. Give your child an ice cube to suck on before taking the medicine; he will hardly taste the medicine when he swallows it.

If your child has difficulty swallowing a pill, put it in a spoonful of applesauce and the pill will go down easily.

Removing gum from hair: There are several techniques you can use to remove gum from hair without cutting the hair. You can pack the gummed hair in ice cubes until the gum has hardened; then gently peel the gum off the hair. Another gum removal technique is to rub cold cream into the hair. With a dry towel, carefully pull down on the gummed strands of hair until the gum comes off. Peanut butter is also effective in removing gum. Massage a small amount of peanut butter into the gum until the gum begins to loosen. Remove with facial tissue.

Kitchen Comforts

I have always dreaded slicing onions because my eyes sting and tear, so I was grateful when my neighbor showed me this trick for eliminating onion-induced tears. Place 2 unlit kitchen matches between your teeth, with the sulfur tips facing out. Keep the matches there while you chop or grate the onions. The sulfur absorbs the onion vapors.

Other ways to avoid tears are to place the onion in the freezer 15 minutes before chopping, and to chop the onions on top of your stove, with the exhaust fan on.

Onions not only make you teary, but also leave an odor on your hands. To remove strong onion and garlic smells, rub your hands with a spoon under cold running water or with a fresh tomato slice.

Here are a couple of tips to prevent accidents from occurring in the kitchen: When you pour hot water from a pot of pasta or vegetables into the sink, keep the cold water running. This helps prevent the steam from scalding you.

Place some dry bread in the broiler. The bread will soak up the fat and prevent grease fires and smoking when you broil.

Shoe Care

I can't tell you how many times I've bought shoes that felt fine when I tried them on, but felt tight after being worn for a few hours. Here is a handy tip to loosen tight-fitting shoes: Dip a cotton ball in rubbing alcohol and rub the area inside the shoe where it feels tight. Put the shoes on immediately and walk around a while. Repeat this process until the shoes feel comfortable.

If your shoes feel too tight around the toes, try crumpling some newspaper into balls. Wet the balls completely and stuff several of them into the toes of the tight shoes. Leave the newspaper balls in place for 3 or 4 days. This should stretch the shoes enough to make them more comfortable.

Here are some shoe shining tips: Use walnut or olive oil to polish shoes, and buff to a shine with a chamois cloth.

Rub your leather shoes with the inside of a banana peel. Wipe clean and polish with a woolen cloth. Or rub shoes with the inside of a freshly cut orange peel. Polish with a soft cloth.

Apply petroleum jelly to leather shoes several times a week and rub them with a soft cloth. The shoes will wear longer and will not need to be polished as often.

Lemon juice gives a great finish to black leather shoes. Spread a few drops of lemon juice on the shoes and massage briskly with a soft cloth.

Book Care

Books are important treasures in my household and can be found lined on bookshelves and piled throughout the house. Books require a certain amount of care to keep them in mint condition.

If water is spilled on a book page, place a blotter on each side of the wet page. Press with a medium-hot iron until the page is dry and smooth.

If a valued book has become a little warped, place it on a flat surface in your bathroom or other humid spot. Place a board on top of the book and leave it for 3 or 4 days.

Here's a great tip for repairing torn pages in books. Place a sheet of waxed paper under the rip to protect the next page. Brush a small amount of white paste on the torn edges and fit the torn pieces together. Place a strip of white tissue paper on the paste so that the entire tear is covered. Weight the paper down until the paste dries. Trim off any excess tissue paper and remove the waxed paper. This works well and doesn't discolor the way cellophane tape does.

Food Storage & Fresheners

My mother baked the most delicious cakes, which remained moist and fresh for days after they were baked. Even when I followed the same recipes, my cakes seemed to dry out quickly. It turns out that her secret was not in the baking but in the storing. She always placed an apple in the cake box with the cake, and this kept the cake moist. These are other handy tips for storing food:

If your bananas get overripe, mash them, add a little lemon juice to prevent browning, and freeze. Use when baking cakes and breads.

Store cottage cheese upside down in its original container to keep it fresh longer.

Peel fresh garlic cloves, then store them in a glass jar filled with safflower oil. The garlic will keep its flavor for a long time because the oil seals it from the air. Remove the garlic when you are ready to use it and you will be left with garlic-flavored oil that is great for cooking or salad dressings.

Store herbs and spices in a dry, cool area so they don't fade and lose their flavor. Refrigerate or freeze spices to preserve their effectiveness.

Wrap onions and potatoes in old pantyhose and hang in a cool place. The pantyhose lets air in, and the vegetables will keep longer.

Coughs

If you are troubled by a cough, there are a number of home-made remedies you can try.

Mix 1 teaspoon of black currant jelly and 1 cup of hot water together. Drink the hot liquid just before going to bed.

For a cough caused by a tickling in your throat, combine 2 teaspoons of apple cider vinegar with 1 glass of water. Take 1 or 2 swallows of the mixture to relieve the tickling feeling.

Peel and slice a turnip. Spread honey on all the slices and let them stand in a bowl for 3 or 4 hours. Take a teaspoon of the syrup that collects at the bottom of the bowl as needed.

Add oil of eucalyptus to the water in your vaporizer to relieve chest congestion and control coughing.

Gently boil 1 medium lemon in a pot of water for 10 minutes. Remove the lemon, halve it, and squeeze out the juice into a glass. Add 2 tablespoon glycerin, stirring well. Fill up the glass with 1 cup honey. Take 1 teaspoon of the mixture as needed to control coughing. Stir before using.

Old-Fashioned Cure-alls

Nothing can make you feel more miserable than a good old-fashioned head cold. Many people believe that a bowl of homemade chicken soup is one of the most effective treatments for colds. There are also a number of herb remedies that usually bring some relief. Try soaking a handful of rosemary tops in warm water until softened. Combine them with a pint of hot cider, ⅛ teaspoon of ground cayenne pepper, and ⅛ teaspoon of ground ginger. Drink the liquid while still hot.

Tea made from ginger and honey is also helpful in relieving cold symptoms, and thyme tea brings relief to sore throats.

My grandfather used a mustard foot bath to clear the congestion of a head cold.

Add 1 tablespoon dry mustard powder to a footbath of 2 gallons of hot water. Soak your feet in the bath for 10 to 15 minutes.

To combat colds, try this remedy: Fill a shallow bowl with honey and add 2 cloves. Make 6 cuts in a lemon and soak it overnight in the honey. Squeeze the remaining lemon juice into the honey and take teaspoons of the mixture when needed to relieve symptoms.

Burns & Sunburns

Serious burns require medical treatment, but for the less-severe burns received by touching hot pans or irons, or by being splattered by hot oil, here are some suggestions to relieve the pain.

Immediately apply cold water or a cold compress to the burn.

Apply slices of unpeeled, raw potato to the area, squeezing the juice onto the burn. Cover with thick honey to keep out the air.

Gently rub the inside of a ripe banana peel over the burn, then wrap the burn in the peel for a few hours.

Break off a piece of stem from an aloe vera plant and squeeze the juice onto the burn.

To relieve the discomfort of sunburns, take a mint-tea bath. Or, pour a quart of low-fat milk into a tub of warm water and soak in it for a half hour.

When you burn your tongue drinking a hot liquid, rinse your mouth repeatedly with cold water.

Headaches

Spearmint and peppermint grows rampant in my back yard, having taken over the entire garden under the kitchen window. I use the fresh mint to prepare mint tea, which is a wonderful remedy for headaches. Dried mint can also be used to prepare this tea, but fresh leaves are preferable.

6 sprigs fresh spearmint or
    peppermint, or 1 teaspoon dried
    mint
1 cup boiling water

Place the mint in a cup and cover with boiling water. Cover with a saucer and steep for 5 minutes. Add a pinch of baking soda, stir, and drink slowly while the tea is still very hot.

Tension headaches can be relieved by resting with fresh mint leaves on your forehead.

There are many different causes of headaches, and many different suggested remedies. Try one of these and see if it works for you.

Make a poultice out of a grated potato or an apple. Place the poultice on your forehead for at least 1 hour.

Rub a small amount of essence of rosemary on your forehead and temples, as well as behind your ears. Repeat the rubbing after a half hour if your headache has not disappeared.

Eat 2 apples a day to prevent headaches.

Stings and Bites

In every family, there always seems to be someone who attracts the majority of biting and stinging insects. In my family, it was my sister. I considered her to be my best insect repellent, because as long as she was around, insects ignored me.

A number of common household items can effectively reduce the pain, itching, and swelling of bites and stings. Try these for relief:

raw onions and potatoes

ammonia

apple cider vinegar

witch hazel

meat tenderizer

toothpaste

wet salt

raw honey
mud
lemon juice
a paste of baking soda and water

If none of these are available when you are stung or bitten, rub the affected area vigorously with any handy green herb. The herb releases chlorophyll, which kills pain. Comfrey, plantain, or savory are the most effective herbs to use but ordinary grass will do. Of course, avoid poison ivy!

Insomnia

A cup of herb tea works wonders if you are unable to get to sleep. Use one of the sleep-inducing herbs for your tea, such as camomile, lemon verbena, red clover, valerian, or birch leaves. These herbs can be used by themselves or in combination to make a relaxing tea.

1/2 cup camomile
1/2 cup valerian
1/2 cup mint

Combine the herbs and store in a bottle or container. Add 1 tablespoon of the herb mixture to a cup of boiling water and steep for 5 minutes. Strain and drink slowly.

Nutmeg can help you relax so that you can sleep. Add half of a crushed nutmeg to a cup of hot water and drink it a half hour before going to bed.

Heat 1½ cups milk gently until warm and pour it into a glass. Stir in 1 teaspoon honey and 1 drop of vanilla extract. Drink the warm mixture just before going to bed.

Honey is a great sleep inducer. Take 1 tablespoon of honey every evening at dinnertime, and you should have less trouble falling asleep at night. If a spoonful of honey doesn't do the trick, try a mixture of 3 teaspoons of apple cider vinegar and 1 cup of honey. Take 2 teaspoons of the mixture when you are getting ready to go to bed. If you still can't sleep after 1 hour, take 2 more teaspoonfuls of the vinegar-honey mixture.

Stomach Ailments

Certain herbal teas are particularly good for the digestion. Camomile tea and mint tea help relieve stomach pains. Red raspberry leaf tea is said to be an effective remedy for morning sickness. Thyme tea helps combat gas pains. The following are suggestions for controlling various stomach ailments.

Constipation: Combine ½ cup olive oil and ½ cup orange juice. Drink in the evening.

Indigestion: Chew 1 teaspoon of dry rolled oats, then swallow them. Or take 1 teaspoon of apricot brandy after your meal.

Nervous stomach: Mix ¼ teaspoon of oregano and ½ teaspoon of marjoram together. Stir the herbs into

1 cup of hot water and steep for 10 minutes. Strain and drink slowly. Repeat every 2 hours, if necessary.

Nausea: Drink a cup of yarrow or ginger tea.

Gas: Crush 1 teaspoon of anise, caraway, dill, or fennel seeds. Combine the crushed seeds and 1 cup of boiling water. Steep for 10 minutes, then strain and drink.

Heartburn: Drink a cup of peppermint tea.

Aches & Pains

There have been times when I overexerted myself, leaving my muscles so sore and stiff that I couldn't move without feeling pain. A massage using a mixture of $\frac{1}{2}$ tablespoon of rosemary oil and 1 cup of olive oil helped relieve the pain of sore muscles.

Make a compress by saturating a wash cloth with 1 cup of warm apple cider vinegar; apply the compress to the achy area for 5 minutes each hour. Rubbing a bruised area with apple cider vinegar once every hour also helps relieve muscle pain.

Comfrey works miracles in relieving the pain and promoting the healing of sprains, strains, and broken bones. Place a comfrey poultice on the injured area, changing it every 2 or 3 hours.

Soaking in a warm ginger tea bath also is soothing for sprains and strains.

Painful muscle cramps can frequently be cured by eating 2 teaspoons of honey at each meal. After about a week, the cramps should disappear.

Here is my favorite remedy for leg cramps: Cut 3 small unpeeled lemons, 1 small grapefruit, and 2 small oranges into small pieces and blend in a blender or food processor. Add 1 teaspoon cream of tartar. Combine 2 tablespoons of the fruit mixture and 2 tablespoons of water and take twice a day. Cover the remaining mixture and refrigerate.

Index

CAUTION

Be _absolutely_ sure you are not allergic to any of the herbs and remedies in this book before trying them.